W9-BHL-294

Pet Dogs

Cecelia H. Brannon

Enslow Publishing
101 W. 23rd Street
Suite 240
New York, NY 10011
USA

enslow.com

Published in 2017 by Enslow Publishing, LLC.
101 W. 23rd Street, Suite 240, New York, NY 10011

Library of Congress Cataloging-in-Publication Data
Names: Brannon, Cecelia H., author.
Title: Pet dogs / Cecelia H. Brannon.
Description: New York, NY : Enslow Publishing, 2017. | Series: All about pets
  | Audience: Age 6-up. | Audience: K to Grade 3. | Includes bibliographical references and index.
Identifiers: LCCN 2015045444| ISBN 9780766076020 (library bound) | ISBN 9780766079182 (pbk.) |
ISBN 9780766075856 (6-pack)
Subjects: LCSH: Dogs—Juvenile literature.
Classification: LCC SF426.5 .B73 2017 | DDC 636.7—dc23
LC record available at http://lccn.loc.gov/2015045444

Printed in Malaysia

To Our Readers: We have done our best to make sure all website addresses in this book were active and appropriate when we went to press. However, the author and the publisher have no control over and assume no liability for the material available on those websites or on any websites they may link to. Any comments or suggestions can be sent by e-mail to customerservice@enslow.com.

Contents

Words to Know

coat   kibble   toys

Dogs make great pets. They are friendly and always happy to see you.

Dogs can learn a lot of fun tricks. They can roll over, raise their paws, and fetch.

A dog's fur is called a coat. This keeps dogs warm and makes them soft to pet.

A dog has a wet nose.
It can smell things humans
cannot smell.

Dogs like to chew on bones. This helps keep their teeth clean.

Dogs have a lot of energy.
They need to play every day.

Dogs eat kibble from a bowl. They should never eat what you eat. People food is bad for them.

When dogs are born, they are called puppies. Puppies are much smaller than their parents. But they will soon be just as big!

Dogs can sleep a lot. They can dream and even snore!

Dogs are happy inside or outside the house. They just want to be with you!

Read More

Hapka, Catherine. *ASPCA Kids: Pet Rescue Club: Too Big to Run*. New York, NY: Reader's Digest. 2015

National Geographic Kids. *Dogs (Look & Learn)*. Washington, DC: National Geographic Publishing. 2014.

Websites

Science Kids
> sciencekids.co.nz/sciencefacts/animals/dog.html

Enchanted Learning
> enchantedlearning.com/subjects/mammals/dog/index.shtml

Index

Guided Reading Level: C
Guided Reading Leveling System is based on the guidelines recommended by Fountas and Pinnell.

Word Count: 152